THE LITTLE BOOK OF

ROB FORD

THE LITTLE BOOK OF
ROB FORD

BY THE UNKNOWN TORONTONIAN

ANANSI

This edition published in 2011 by
House of Anansi Press Inc.
110 Spadina Avenue, Suite 801
Toronto, ON, M5V 2K4
Tel. 416-363-4343 • Fax 416-363-1017
www.anansi.ca

Distributed in Canada by
HarperCollins Canada Ltd.
1995 Markham Road
Scarborough, ON, M1B 5M8
Toll free tel. 1-800-387-0117

Distributed in the United States by
Publishers Group West
1700 Fourth Street
Berkeley, CA 94710
Toll free tel. 1-800-788-3123

House of Anansi Press is committed to protecting our natural environment. As part of our efforts, this book is printed on paper that contains 100% post-consumer recycled fibres, is acid-free, and is processed chlorine-free.

15 14 13 12 11 1 2 3 4 5

LIBRARY AND ARCHIVES CANADA CATALOGUING IN PUBLICATION

Unknown Torontonian
The little book of Rob Ford / the Unknown Torontonian.

ISBN 978-1-77089-007-7

1. Ford, Rob, 1969– — Humour. 2. Ford, Rob, 1969– — Quotations.
3. Toronto (Ont.) — Politics and government — 21st century — Humour.
4. Toronto (Ont.) — Politics and government — 21st century — Quotations, maxims, etc. 5. Malapropisms. I. Title.

FC3097.3.U55 2011 971.3'541092 C2011-900293-0

Library of Congress Control Number: 2010919129

Cover design: Alysia Shewchuk • Text design and typesetting: Alysia Shewchuk

Canada Council for the Arts Conseil des Arts du Canada

ONTARIO ARTS COUNCIL
CONSEIL DES ARTS DE L'ONTARIO

We acknowledge for their financial support of our publishing program the Canada Council for the Arts, the Ontario Arts Council, and the Government of Canada through the Canada Book Fund.

Printed and bound in Canada

CONTENTS

INTRODUCTION

THERE HAS NEVER BEEN A TORONTO POLITICIAN LIKE ROB FORD. Or rather, there hasn't been one for a long time. In the age of PR teams, talking points, and focus groups, Rob Ford is a throwback to another era, when politicians were blunt and when plain-speaking — not political spin — was the rule.

His candidacy for mayor of Toronto was the classic underdog story, and his victory was, at first, unforeseen by pundits, pollsters, most journalists, and just about everyone outside of the Ford campaign. A Toronto resident could reasonably have woken up on the morning after the election and wondered, "Who did we just elect?"

Consider this book the answer to that question. It's a primer on all things Rob Ford, straight from the hip and in his own words.

ON POLITICS

If you can't stand the heat, get out of the kitchen and don't get into public life.

I'm a businessman . . . I know how to create jobs, I know how to meet a payroll. I'm going to stop playing games like everyone else plays in the provincial government and the municipal government. Let's get the job done. It comes down to customer service.

There is no trick, there is no magic formula. All it is, is door-knocking, hard work, and anyone has a chance at being elected.

It's teamwork with hundreds of employees, and that's where my leadership skills come into play. I know how to build an empire.

Municipal politics affects your life way more than any level does.

I'm just focused on my message and making sure I deliver the message as directly as possible.

People at least know that
my message is crystal clear.

ON TAXES AND TAXPAYERS

I just know the taxpayers want the gravy train to come to an end, and that Rob Ford's the guy to do it . . . I'm going to put an end to the wasteful spending and, uh, you know, stop the gravy train and — sorry, I'm being distracted — and that's pretty well it.

We're going to stop the wasteful spending, and not have $12,000 retirement parties, and, you know, all the other nonsense that's been going on for seven years. Anyways, I gotta let you go here and, uh, I can't talk to you right now. I'm on a very tight schedule, so I hate to be rude, but I've got to let you go and we can chat another time. Really nice talking to you, all the best, bye-bye.

I like heritage as much as the next person, but can we afford to hand out $230,000 in heritage grants right now? No, we can't.

A grant, by the way, is free money.

We're spending $3 million, Hydro is, and we're making $3,000 a year, and they're saying we're making money. Do the math: it takes a thousand years to break even.

This is the definition of insanity, but this is the city council that we're dealing with.

[On the solar panel installation at the CNE]

If you have a problem with any issue in this city, I'll guarantee you call my office — you can call me at home, 233-6934, or you can call me at City Hall, 397-9255 — and I will return your call and I will get the job done.

I'm not worried about what people do in their private life. I look out for taxpayers' money.

It's just not fair to force you to cut back on essentials so politicians can enjoy their perks.

ON CITY HALL

It's time to stop the gravy train.

We will reduce the size of city council.

Giving the mayor more power for this council is like giving criminals free guns.

There is a lot of waste at City Hall — everyone knows this. Even my competitors are finally admitting this.

Right now I can't say I'm really proud of being part of council in Toronto, with all the money being spent and the high taxes.

I wouldn't trust them [fellow councillors] as far as I could throw them.

I've put on parties, we all have parties. I don't go out and rent bunny suits and Dalmatian suits. And stilt-walking.

[On expenses submitted by fellow councillors]

You have to have business people running the city. People knowing how to create a job, knowing how to meet a payroll, and knowing everything about customer service. Customer service is number one in business, and it's missing down at City Hall.

When I'm mayor, we're not going to have these so-called in-camera meetings unless they're absolutely imperative. But a lot of these meetings are not imperative. But that's where a lot of skullduggery goes on, that's where a lot of scams go on.

This city has twenty-two MPs, twenty-two MPPs, and twenty-two school trustees. We do not need forty-four councillors down at City Hall.

ON CITY PLANNING

The city will be spotless. We're going to make sure it's clean. And it's going to be safe. And we're going to make sure the city's, um, Toronto's going to be on the map by the time the Pan Am Games get here [in 2015], that's for sure.

There will not be graffiti. Give me six months, and I will guarantee there will not be graffiti.

This is an insult to my constituents
to even think about having a homeless
shelter in their ward. And you want me to
have a public meeting about this?
Why don't we have a public lynching?

People do not want more government housing in the City of Toronto. They want roads fixed, more police presence, but they don't want more government housing that will depreciate the value of their property.

I don't like all the graffiti. The dirt. The long grass and weeds. And all that sort of stuff. I hate that stuff. And I know I'm going to get it all cleaned up when I'm mayor.

I'm going to take it year by year. I talked to staff this year, and they seem to think we can come up with a 0 % [property] tax increase and not have any major service cuts.

ON TRANSPORTATION

The roads are worse than they've ever been,
and I've been all over the place.

People do not want streetcars in this city, they want subways. If you get behind a streetcar, you're stuck! Enough with the streetcars!

Gridlock creates pollution.
It keeps you away from your families.

What I compare bike lanes to is swimming with the sharks. Sooner or later, you're going to get bitten. And every year we have dozens of people that get hit by cars or trucks. Well, no wonder. Roads are built for buses, cars, and trucks. Not for people on bikes. And my heart bleeds for them when I hear someone gets killed, but it's their own fault at the end of the day.

I am a huge fan of subways and buses.
Streetcars — I'm not in favour of streetcars.

Cyclists are a pain in the ass.

Like it or not, cars are here to stay. Let's deal with it. It's time to stop the war on cars.

It doesn't make sense having bike lanes in the suburbs. I call them lanes to nowhere.

If you build it [Sheppard subway extension],
they will come.

Transit City is over, ladies and gentlemen.

ON DRUGS AND ALCOHOL

I don't use drugs. I'm not in that scene.

What does OxyContin go for on the street, so I have an idea?

I'll try, buddy, I'll try. I don't know this shit [OxyContin], but I'll fucking try to find it.

Why don't you go on the street
and score it [OxyContin]?

If you're not doing needles and you're not gay, you won't get AIDS, probably.

The reason I forgot about the marijuana charge . . . is because that same evening I was charged with failing to give a breath sample.

I went for Valentine's with my wife, we had a couple of bottles of wine. I wasn't drunk, but maybe I shouldn't have been driving. Not bottles . . . We shared a couple of litres of wine.

We all make mistakes. It was bad. I was drinking and driving. But a lot of people drink and drive. I got caught.

They pulled me over. I was with my wife. They found one joint in my back pocket.

I think the laws are appropriate, and I'm not one to say we should legalize marijuana. I've never said that, and I wouldn't want to see that happen.

I completely forgot about it until you mentioned it right now. You think I'm BS'ing you, but I'm not. It completely, totally slipped my mind.

[On Ford's failure to disclose charges of possession of marijuana in 1999]

ON DIVERSITY

It's not Bay Street or the Albany Club that's behind me. It's Main Street.

We can't even deal with the 2.5 million people in this city. I think it's more important that we take care of the people now before we start bringing in more.

Those Oriental people work like dogs. They work their hearts out, they are workers non-stop. They sleep beside their machines.

And to this day I apologize to them, and they are a very, very hard-working culture. Very. I went to Hong Kong, I went to Taiwan, I've been to Japan, I've been to Korea. I've seen how hard Asians work.

Gino-boy.

[On Councillor Giorgio Mammoliti; Ford denied making this statement.]

I don't understand. Number one, I don't understand a transgender. I don't understand: is it a guy dressed up as a girl or a girl dressed up as a guy? And we're funding this for, I don't know, what does it say here? We're giving them $3,210?

I have no problem giving money out to physically or mentally handicapped children or seniors, but spending $5,000 on this video [about homosexuality in Toronto's South Asian community] is disgusting. It is absolutely disgusting to spend this amount of money on this, whatever it was called, video.

ON SPORTS AND RECREATION

I'm a coach. I'm a football coach.

Summer football is for all ages . . . You can call my office, and I can sign you up for a team.

A kid misses a practice, he doesn't play in the game. We go three o'clock to six, every day. Doesn't matter if it's cold or raining. We teach life lessons here.

This is ridiculous. You're paying someone $2,500 to sit in a park and bird-watch?

The purpose of marathons is
to create revenue for charities.

I ran about three miles today, little tired, but we're doing it every day, we're doing well. Just curling and doing some bench, trying to stay in shape . . . My max bench is probably about 250.

Even if you don't like it or you like it, this is . . . it's a win-win situation. And again, it benefits everyone. It creates jobs, tourism — it's restaurants, hotels, everyone benefits from it. I want my MMA [Mixed Martial Arts]!

I've been a huge fan. Don [Cherry] is exactly what you see is what you get.

ON YOUTH

The best social program is a job.

It's great having police officers in schools. The kids feel more comfortable, and then outside they'll help you with your homework, they'll help you with the sports, they'll help you with your music, whatever you need. The police officer is there, and if they can't help you, they'll bring in their friends and it's one big happy family.

Eventually I want every high school to have police officers in their school. It makes sense. It keeps our schools safe. The kids respect it.

These kids are good kids.
They just need some guidance in life.

I'm doing my share [for at-risk/troubled youth], I'm carrying a lot already . . . If I could do theatre, I'd do everything.

We have to have that mixture of both education and fun, and when you're having fun, you learn a lot better.

Let me tell you what Rob Ford's character is about: it's about integrity. It's about helping kids get off the street, helping thousands of kids get out of gangs, putting my own money where my mouth is. I don't talk the talk, I walk the walk.

We have to keep the youth busy, and when you're busy, you're staying out of trouble — everybody knows that.

When Vince Carter was playing for the Raptors, he built a million-dollar basketball court for the kids in a very high-needs area . . . It didn't cost the taxpayers a dime . . . To this day, that basketball court is packed. It really helps out that whole neighbourhood.

Look at my leadership skills with dealing with youths. I have the Rob Ford Football Foundation. I take kids out of jail, out of gangs. I've been doing it for eighteen years.

ON FAMILY

It's the happiest time in my life when my family's all together . . . That's all I wanted from the beginning and that's what I have now.

My kids and my family are
first and foremost.

I'm not guilty and I'm glad this is over.
I'm glad to be back with my family.

[On being cleared of domestic
assault charges]

As my father taught me:
if you look after the pennies,
the dollars will look after themselves.

When I said "working like a dog," [when] I was brought up, my father told me every day to "Get out of bed and work like a dog, son." A dog means you're a hard worker.

Before [my father] passed away in 2006, he knew I was going to be mayor.

ON THE OFFENSIVE

Go ahead, take me to jail.

Who the fuck do you think you are?
Are you a fucking teacher?

[Ford to a couple at a Maple Leafs game]

Do you want your little wife to go over to Iran and get raped and shot?

[Ford to a couple at a Maple Leafs game]

Right-wing commie bastard.

[Ford to a couple at a Maple Leafs game]

She's a joke. She's a waste of time.
A waste of skin.

[On Councillor Gloria Lindsay Luby]

They've been attacking me first thing all the time. I just want to put my record in politics against anyone else's.

[On fellow mayoral candidates]

What did you just say? You called me a fat fuck, right now, you did, you just did. Are you gonna lie about that? Are you gonna lie about that, Barber? Are you gonna lie about that?

[Addressing *Globe and Mail* columnist John Barber]

ON THE DEFENSIVE

I'm not perfect.
I have never claimed to be perfect.

I'm exonerated. I'm not guilty.
I'm just glad this is over.

[On domestic violence charges
being dropped]

We all have problems behind closed doors, but mine are a bit more exposed than everyone else's.

It's humiliating. Your name is spotted through the news in a derogatory way.

[On media attention surrounding domestic violence charges]

I apologized to the Asian community for calling them Orientals. I did not know that was a racist comment.

Was it wrong? Absolutely it was wrong and I made a mistake. You learn by your mistakes.

[On 1999 posession of marijuana charges, which were eventually dropped]

It was nothing. It wasn't a major issue.
There's more serious things in life.

[On 1999 posession of marijuana charges,
which were eventually dropped]

I can take the criticism.

FORD ON FORD

I consider myself a fiscal conservative and a social liberal.

I'm caring.

"He did what he said he was going to do." That's what you're going to see after four years of Rob Ford being there.

I'm not one to be phony or anything.

I admit I'm not a smooth talker, a polished speaker. But a lot of people like that. As soon as you're a smooth talker, something's fishy.

I speak in terms that people can understand, and answer the question as directly as I can.

Maybe I'm a perfectionist.

I'm just digesting my food. That's a lot I ate.

That's the way I am
and that's the way I'm going to be.

Only time will tell. You'll see how I work.

THE WORLD ON FORD

"The defendant approached me and took all his money and threw it on the ground. The defendant was acting nervous. When the defendant spoke to me, I could smell a strong odour of an alcoholic beverage on his breath. His eyes were bloodshot."

— Miami-Dade police officer's arrest report, February 15, 1999

"I think people are starting to ask themselves, 'Is this the kind of guy who we want to run our city?'"

— John Wright, Senior Vice President, Ipsos-Reid

"We can't have Rob Ford run the city."

— Judy Sgro, Liberal MP

"I don't think Rob has a chance of winning."

— Rob Oliphant, Liberal MP

"Rob Ford is bananas."

— *Eye Weekly*

"He sees himself as the norm, and it is so frightening to think that he might lead a city whose motto is, 'Diversity is our strength.'"

— Councillor Pam McConnell

"'Never get into a wrestling match with a pig. You both get dirty, and the pig likes it.'"

— *Globe and Mail* columnist John Barber, quoting United States Senator John McCain, in response to his 2005 shouting match with Rob Ford

"When I heard he had decided to run for mayor, I wondered if he knew it was a full-time job."

— Councillor Adam Vaughan

"He is the Walmart of politicians."

— *Toronto Life*

"I say he's going to be the greatest mayor this city has ever, ever seen, as far as I'm concerned. You can put that in your pipe, you left-wing kooks."

— Don Cherry

BIBLIOGRAPHY

ON POLITICS

Page 3: Vincent, Donovan, and Robin Doolittle. "Lawyer Defends Ford's Actions." *Toronto Star*. March 28, 2008. <http://www.thestar.com/News/GTA/article/404786>

Page 4: Toronto mayoral debate, May 19, 2010. <http://www.youtube.com watch?v=XOzdETJq_Kc&feature=related>

Page 5: Ford campaign video, February 13, 2010. <http://www.youtube.com/watch?v=lXO_sjBXqNQ&feature=related>

Page 6: To reporters after announcing his mayoral candidacy, March 25, 2010. <http://www.youtube.com/watch?v=e7AgBEQferU&feature=related>

Page 7: CBC interview with Evan Solomon after Toronto mayoral debate, October 5, 2010. <http://www.youtube.com/watch?v=jbhOPF5pzQw&feature=related>

Page 8: Kohler, Nicholas. "The Political Genius of Rob Ford." *Maclean's*, October 12, 2010. <http://www2.macleans.ca/2010/10/12/the-political-genius-of-rob-ford/>

Page 9: CP24 Mayoral debate, October 21, 2010. <http://www.youtube.com/watch?v=iWAyP-3W9Bw&feature=related>

ON TAXES AND TAXPAYERS

Page 13: Interview on "As It Happens," CBC Radio, October 26, 2010. <http://www.youtube.com/watch?v=mHJGR4i7fhw&feature=related>

Page 14: CBC interview with Evan Solomon after Toronto mayoral debate, October 5, 2010. <http://www.youtube.com/watch?v=jbhOPF5pzQw&feature=related>

Page 15: Interview on Talk Radio AM640, February 11, 2010. <http://www.youtube.com/watch?v=ZOZ7B4LKUVw&feature=related>

Page 16: Interview on Talk Radio AM640, February 11, 2010. <http://www.youtube.com/watch?v=ZOZ7B4LKUVw&feature=related>

Page 17: Interview on Talk Radio AM640, February 4, 2010. <http://www.youtube.com/watch?v=2TdmuFHROyg&feature=related>

Page 18: Interview on Talk Radio AM640, February 4, 2010.<http://www.youtube.com/watch?v=2TdmuFHROyg&feature=related>

Page 19: Interview on Talk Radio AM640, February 25, 2010. <http://www.youtube.com/watch?v=FTJowVN_aWw>

Page 20: Daubs, Katie. "Rob Ford's Toronto: Fewer Wildcat Strikes, More Subways." *Toronto Star*. October 26, 2010.

Page 21: Rob Ford campaign video, September 27, 2010. <http://www.youtube.com/watch?v=ry1-xZIx_Zw&feature=related>

ON CITY HALL

Page 25: Rob Ford campaign video, September 27, 2010. <http://www.youtube.com/watch?v=ry1-xZIx_Zw&feature=related>

Page 26: Rob Ford campaign video, September 27, 2010. <http://www.youtube.com/watch?v=ry1-xZIx_Zw&feature=related>

Page 27: Mahoney, Jill. "Rob Ford and a Decade of Controversy." *Globe and Mail.* August 19, 2010. <http://www.theglobeandmail.com/news/national/toronto/rob-ford-and-a-decade-of-controversy/article1678543/page1/>

Page 28: Rob Ford campaign video, September 27, 2010. <http://www.youtube.com/watch?v=ry1-xZIx_Zw&feature=related>

Page 29: Kohler, Nicholas. "The Political Genius of Rob Ford." *Maclean's.* October 12, 2010. <http://www2.macleans.ca/2010/10/12/the-political-genius-of-rob-ford/>

Page 30: Interview on Talk Radio AM640, February 25, 2010. <http://www.youtube.com/watch?v=FTJowVN_aWw>

Page 31: Interview on Talk Radio AM640, March 20, 2010. <http://www.youtube.com/watch?v=vnp_N6DuLPo&NR=1>

Page 32: To reporters after announcing his mayoral candidacy, March 25, 2010. <http://www.youtube.com/watch?v=e7AgBEQferU&feature=related>

Page 33: "Town Crier" editorial meeting, August 24, 2010. <http://www.youtube.com/watch?v=zEwtEa5SBIs&feature=related>

Page 34: To reporters after announcing candidacy, March 25, 2010 <http://www.youtube.com/watch?v=uYsK6nRubqQ&feature=related>

ON CITY PLANNING

Page 37: Kohler, Nicholas. "The Political Genius of Rob Ford." *Maclean's.* October 12, 2010. <http://www2.macleans.ca/2010/10/12/the-political-genius-of-rob-ford/>

Page 38: To reporters on October 8, 2010. <http://www.youtube.com/watch?v=iWAyP-3W9Bw&feature=related>

Page 39: Mahoney, Jill. "Rob Ford and a Decade of Controversy." *Globe and Mail.* August 19, 2010. <http://www.theglobeandmail.com/news/national/toronto/rob-ford-and-a-decade-of-controversy/article1678543/page1/>

Page 40: Mahoney, Jill. "Rob Ford and a Decade of Controversy." *Globe and Mail.* August 19, 2010. <http://www.theglobeandmail.com/news/national/toronto/rob-ford-and-a-decade-of-controversy/article1678543/page1/>

Page 41: Kohler, Nicholas. "The Political Genius of Rob Ford." *Maclean's.* October 12, 2010. <http://www2.macleans.ca/2010/10/12/the-political-genius-of-rob-ford/>

Page 42: Alcoba, Natalie. "Can Rob Ford Do All That?" *National Post.* December 4, 2010. <http://news.nationalpost.com/2010/12/05/can-rob-ford-do-all-that/>

ON TRANSPORTATION

Page 45: City council debate on Jarvis Street improvements, May 25, 2009. <http://www.youtube.com/watch?v=xwxiv2aznB0&feature=related>

Page 46: Kohler, Nicholas. "The Political Genius of Rob Ford." *Maclean's*. October 12, 2010. <http://www2.macleans.ca/2010/10/12/the-political-genius-of-rob-ford/>

Page 47: Rob Ford campaign video, September 7, 2010. <http://youtube.com/watch?v=_xfsIj6gYAw&NR=1>

Page 48: Mahoney, Jill. "Rob Ford and a Decade of Controversy." *Globe and Mail*. August 19, 2010. <http://www.theglobeandmail.com/news/national/toronto/rob-ford-and-a-decade-of-controversy/article1678543/page1/>

Page 49: Rob Ford telephone town hall, May 7, 2010. <http://www.youtube.com/watch?v=iWeNROlGW8A&NR=1>

Page 50: City council debate on Jarvis Street improvements, May 25, 2009. <http://www.youtube.com/watch?v=xwxiv2aznB0&feature=related>

Page 51: Rob Ford campaign video, September 7, 2010. <http://www.youtube.com/watch?v=_xfsIj6gYAw&NR=1>

Page 52: Mayoral debate in Scarborough, March 29, 2010. <http://www.youtube.com/watch?v=aF_NgbtUR6E>

Page 53: Alcoba, Natalie. "Ford's Plan Aims to Stop 'War on Cars.'" *National Post*. September 9, 2010. <http://www.nationalpost.com/todays-paper/Ford+plan+aims+stop+cars/3498533/story.html>

Page 54: "Rob Ford: Transit City Is Over." CBC News. December 1, 2010. <http://www.cbc.ca/canada/toronto/story/2010/12/01/toronto-ford.html>

ON DRUGS AND ALCOHOL

Page 57: Jenkins, Jonathan, and Rob Lamberti. "Ford Dodges Pot Bust in Florida." *Toronto Sun*. August 18, 2010. <http://www.torontosun.com/news/torontoandgta/2010/08/18/15067206.html>

Page 58: Conversation with Dieter Doneit-Henderson, recorded June 4, 2010. *Toronto Sun*. June 17, 2010. <http://www.youtube.com/watch?v=7FaMlzEnHmE&feature=related>

Page 59: Conversation with Dieter Doneit-Henderson, recorded June 4, 2010. *Toronto Sun*. June 17, 2010. <http://www.youtube.com/watch?v=7FaMlzEnHmE&feature=related>

Page 60: Conversation with Dieter Doneit-Henderson, recorded June 4, 2010. *Toronto Sun*. June 17, 2010. <http://www.youtube.com/watch?v=7FaMlzEnHmE&feature=related>

Page 61: Mahoney, Jill. "Rob Ford and a Decade of Controversy." *Globe and Mail*. August 19, 2010. <http://www.theglobeandmail.com/news/national/toronto/rob-ford-and-a-decade-of-controversy/article1678543/page1/>

Page 62: Mahoney, Jill. "Rob Ford and a Decade of Controversy." *Globe and Mail*. August 19, 2010. <http://www.theglobeandmail.com/news/national/toronto/rob-ford-and-a-decade-of-controversy/article1678543/page1/>

Page 63: Mahoney, Jill. "Rob Ford and a Decade of Controversy." *Globe and Mail*. August 19, 2010. <http://www.theglobeandmail.com/news/national/toronto/rob-ford-and-a-decade-of-controversy/article1678543/page1/>

Page 64: Kohler, Nicholas. "The Political Genius of Rob Ford." *Maclean's*. October 12, 2010. <http://www2.macleans.ca/2010/10/12/the-political-genius-of-rob-ford/>

Page 65: Jenkins, Jonathan, and Rob Lamberti. "Ford Dodges Pot Bust in Florida." *Toronto Sun*. August 18, 2010. <http://www.torontosun.com/news/torontoandgta/2010/08/18/15067206.html>

Page 66: Jenkins, Jonathan, and Rob Lamberti. "Ford Dodges Pot Bust in Florida." *Toronto Sun*. August 18, 2010. <http://www.torontosun.com/news/torontoandgta/2010/08/18/15067206.html>

Page 67: Mahoney, Jill. "Rob Ford and a Decade of Controversy." *Globe and Mail*. August 19, 2010. <http://www.theglobeandmail.com/news/national/toronto/rob-ford-and-a-decade-of-controversy/article1678543/page1/>

ON DIVERSITY

Page 71: Hannon, Gerald. "Mr. Popular: Why Rob Ford's Winning Over Toronto." *Toronto Life*. September 29, 2010. <http://www.torontolife.com/daily/informer/from-print-edition-informer/2010/09/29/mr-popular-why-rob-ford-winning-over-toronto/?page=3>

Page 72: Alcoba, Natalie. "Mayoral Candidate Rob Ford Defends Controversial Immigration Comments." *National Post*. August 18, 2010. <http://news.nationalpost.com/2010/08/18/mayoral-candidate-rob-ford-defends-controversial-immigration-comments/>

Page 73: Mahoney, Jill. "Rob Ford and a Decade of Controversy." *Globe and Mail*. August 19, 2010. <http://www.theglobeandmail.com/news/national/toronto/rob-ford-and-a-decade-of-controversy/article1678543/page1/>

Page 74: Interview on *The Agenda with Steve Paikin*. September 7, 2010. <http://www.youtube.com/watch?v=GIA2du-qUP4&feature=channel>

Page 75: Mahoney, Jill. "Rob Ford and a Decade of Controversy." *Globe and Mail*. August 19, 2010. <http://www.theglobeandmail.com/news/national/toronto/rob-ford-and-a-decade-of-controversy/article1678543/page1/>

Page 76: Mahoney, Jill. "Rob Ford and a Decade of Controversy." *Globe and Mail*. August 19, 2010. <http://www.theglobeandmail.com/news/national/toronto/rob-ford-and-a-decade-of-controversy/article1678543/page1/>

Page 77: Mahoney, Jill. "Rob Ford and a Decade of Controversy." *Globe and Mail*. August 19, 2010. <http://www.theglobeandmail.com/news/national/toronto/rob-ford-and-a-decade-of-controversy/article1678543/page1/>

ON SPORTS AND RECREATION

Page 81: Interview on "As It Happens," CBC Radio, October 26, 2010. <http://www.youtube.com/watch?v=mHJGR4i7fhw&feature=related>

Page 82: Rob Ford campaign video, February 4, 2010. <http://www.youtube.com/watch?v=CJDmB808pO4&feature=related>

Page 83: Hannon, Gerald. "Mr. Popular: Why Rob Ford's Winning Over Toronto." *Toronto Life*. September 29, 2010. <http://www.torontolife.com/daily/informer/from-print-edition-informer/2010/09/29/mr-popular-why-rob-ford-winning-over-toronto/?page=3>

Page 84: Interview on Talk Radio AM640, February 11, 2010. <http://www.youtube.com/watch?v=ZOZ7B4LKUVw&feature=related>

Page 85: Rob Ford campaign video, February 4, 2010. <http://www.youtube.com/watch?v=6eX66AjIXC8&feature=related>

Page 86: Rob Ford campaign video, June 23, 2010. <http://www.youtube.com/watch?v=G-6oA_KV0-g&feature=related>

Page 87: Rob Ford campaign video, March 23, 2010. <http://www.youtube.com/watch?v=APiJ3zMtP7s&feature=related>

Page 88: Rider, David. "Don Cherry Rips 'Left-Wing Pinkos' at Council Inaugural." *Toronto Star*. December 7, 2010. <http://www.thestar.com/news/article/902903>

ON YOUTH

Page 91: Toronto mayoral debate, May 6, 2010. <http://www.youtube.com/watch?v=zf-l0Tpyrgw>

Page 92: Toronto mayoral debate, May 6, 2010. <http://www.youtube.com/watch?v=qnT1jrebSa4&feature=related>

Page 93: Rob Ford campaign video, June 3, 2010. <http://www.youtube.com/watch?v=hFQinLU-mKc>

Page 94: Toronto mayoral debate, October 5, 2010. <http://www.youtube.com/watch?v=u8o2H2N5VtM&feature=related>

Page 95: Toronto mayoral debate, October 5, 2010. <http://www.youtube.com/watch?v=u8o2H2N5VtM&feature=related>

Page 96: Toronto mayoral debate, May 6, 2010. <http://www.youtube.com/watch?v=qnT1jrebSa4&feature=related>

Page 97: Toronto mayoral debate, May 18, 2010. <http://www.youtube.com/watch?v=a5-JxRiKlnY&feature=related>

Page 98: Toronto mayoral debate, May 6, 2010 <http://www.youtube.com/watch?v=qnT1jrebSa4&feature=related>

Page 99: Hart House Youth debate, September 2, 2010. <http://www.youtube.com/watch?v=a5H5qJTOmG4&feature=related>

Page 100: Interview on *The Agenda with Steve Paikin*. September 7, 2010. <http://www.youtube.com/watch?v=GIA2du-qUP4&feature=channel>

ON FAMILY

Page 103: Mahoney, Jill. "Rob Ford and a Decade of Controversy." *Globe and Mail*. August 19, 2010. <http://www.theglobeandmail.com/news/national/toronto/rob-ford-and-a-decade-of-controversy/article1678543/page1/>

Page 104: Freed, Dale Anne. "Rob Ford's Assault Charge Withdrawn." *Toronto Star.* May 21, 2008. <http://www.thestar.com/news/gta/article/428338>

Page 105: Freed, Dale Anne. "Rob Ford's Assault Charge Withdrawn." *Toronto Star.* May 21, 2008. <http://www.thestar.com/news/gta/article/428338>

Page 106: Rob Ford campaign video, September 27, 2010. <http://www.youtube.com/watch?v=ry1-xZIx_Zw&feature=related>

Page 107: Mahoney, Jill. "Rob Ford and a Decade of Controversy." *Globe and Mail.* August 19, 2010. <http://www.theglobeandmail.com/news/national/toronto/rob-ford-and-a-decade-of-controversy/article1678543/page1/>

Page 108: Kohler, Nicholas. "The Political Genius of Rob Ford." *Maclean's.* October 12, 2010. <http://www2.macleans.ca/2010/10/12/the-political-genius-of-rob-ford/>

ON THE OFFENSIVE

Page 111: Mahoney, Jill. "Rob Ford and a Decade of Controversy." *Globe and Mail.* August 19, 2010. <http://www.theglobeandmail.com/news/national/toronto/rob-ford-and-a-decade-of-controversy/article1678543/page1/>

Page 112: Mahoney, Jill. "Rob Ford and a Decade of Controversy." *Globe and Mail.* August 19, 2010. <http://www.theglobeandmail.com/news/national/toronto/rob-ford-and-a-decade-of-controversy/article1678543/page1/>

Page 113: Mahoney, Jill. "Rob Ford and a Decade of Controversy." *Globe and Mail.* August 19, 2010. <http://www.theglobeandmail.com/news/national/toronto/rob-ford-and-a-decade-of-controversy/article1678543/page1/>

Page 114: Hannon, Gerald. "Mr. Popular: Why Rob Ford's Winning Over Toronto." *Toronto Life.* September 29, 2010. <http://www.torontolife.com/daily/informer/from-print-edition-informer/2010/09/29/mr-popular-why-rob-ford-winning-over-toronto/?page=3>

Page 115: Mahoney, Jill. "Rob Ford and a Decade of Controversy." *Globe and Mail.* August 19, 2010. <http://www.theglobeandmail.com/news/national/toronto/rob-ford-and-a-decade-of-controversy/article1678543/page1/>

Page 116: CBC interview with Evan Solomon after Toronto mayoral debate, October 5, 2010. <http://www.youtube.com/watch?v=jbhOPF5pzQw&feature>

Page 117: An exchange with *Globe and Mail* columnist John Barber in the 2005 documentary, *Hogtown: The Politics of Policing.* <http://www.youtube.com/watch?v=z8EpSdyB0zY>

ON THE DEFENSIVE

Page 121: Mahoney, Jill. "Rob Ford and a Decade of Controversy." *Globe and Mail.* August 19, 2010. <http://www.theglobeandmail.com/news/national/toronto/rob-ford-and-a-decade-of-controversy/article1678543/page1/>

Page 122: Freed, Dale Anne. "Rob Ford's Assault Charge Withdrawn." *Toronto Star.* May 21, 2008. <http://www.thestar.com/news/gta/article/428338>

Page 123: City News staff. "Charges of Domestic Assault Withdrawn Against Councillor Rob Ford." Citytv.com. May 21, 2008. <http://www.citytv.com/toronto/citynews/news/local/article/1925--charges-of-domestic-assault-withdrawn-against-councillor-rob-ford>

Page 124: Freed, Dale Anne. "Rob Ford's Assault Charge Withdrawn." *Toronto Star.* May 21, 2008. <http://www.thestar.com/news/gta/article/428338>

Page 125: Interview on *The Agenda with Steve Paikin*. September 7, 2010. <http://www.youtube.com/watch?v=GIA2du-qUP4&feature=channel>

Page 126: Jenkins, Jonathan, and Rob Lamberti. "Ford Dodges Pot Bust in Florida." *Toronto Sun*. August 18, 2010. <http://www.torontosun.com/news/torontoandgta/2010/08/18/15067206.html>

Page 127: Jenkins, Jonathan, and Rob Lamberti. "Ford Dodges Pot Bust in Florida." *Toronto Sun*. August 18, 2010. <http://www.torontosun.com/news/torontoandgta/2010/08/18/15067206.html>

Page 128: Toronto city council debate, May 25, 2009. <http://www.youtube.com/watch?v=xwxiv2aznB0&feature=related>

FORD ON FORD

Page 131: Interview on *The Agenda with Steve Paikin*. September 7, 2010. <http://www.youtube.com/watch?v=GIA2du-qUP4&feature=channel>

Page 132: Toronto mayoral debate, May 19, 2010. <http://www.youtube.com/watch?v=a5-JxRiKlnY&feature=related>

Page 133: Campaign speech, October 12, 2010 <http://www.youtube.com/watch?v=J0p2Twr2qRI&NR=1>

Page 134: Interview on *The Agenda with Steve Paikin*. September 7, 2010. <http://www.youtube.com/watch?v=GIA2du-qUP4&feature=channel>

Page 135: Kohler, Nicholas. "The Political Genius of Rob Ford." *Maclean's*. October 12, 2010. <http://www2.macleans.ca/2010/10/12/the-political-genius-of-rob-ford/>

Page 136: Kohler, Nicholas. "The Political Genius of Rob Ford." *Maclean's*. October 12, 2010. <http://www2.macleans.ca/2010/10/12/the-political-genius-of-rob-ford/>

Page 137: Kohler, Nicholas. "The Political Genius of Rob Ford." *Maclean's*. October 12, 2010. <http://www2.macleans.ca/2010/10/12/the-political-genius-of-rob-ford/>

Page 138: Kohler, Nicholas. "The Political Genius of Rob Ford." *Maclean's*. October 12, 2010. <http://www2.macleans.ca/2010/10/12/the-political-genius-of-rob-ford/>

Page 139: Interview on Talk Radio AM640, February 25, 2010. <http://www.youtube.com/watch?v=FTJowVN_aWw>

Page 140: To reporters on October 8, 2010. <http://www.youtube.com/watch?v=YR-UjLuHoIY&feature=related>

THE WORLD ON FORD

Page 143: Dempsey, Amy. "'Go Ahead Take Me to Jail,' Rob Ford Told Police." *Toronto Star.* August 19, 2010. < http://www.thestar.com/news/gta/article/849744--go-ahead-take-me-to-jail-ford-told-police>

Page 144: Grant, Kelly. "Ford's Drunk Driving Conviction Could Steer His Campaign into the Ditch." *Globe and Mail.* August 19, 2010. <http://www.theglobeandmail.com/news/national/toronto/fords-drunk-driving-conviction-could-steer-his-campaign-into-the-ditch/article1678316/>

Page 145: Raphael, Mitchel. "Mitchel Raphael on Who Said What, Who Dissed Who, the First Day Back." *Maclean's.* September 30, 2010. <http://www2.macleans.ca/2010/09/30/mitchel-raphael-on-who-said-what-who-dissed-who-the-first-day-back/>

Page 146: Raphael, Mitchel. "Mitchel Raphael on Who Said What, Who Dissed Who, the First Day Back." *Maclean's.* September 30, 2010. <http://www2.macleans.ca/2010/09/30/mitchel-raphael-on-who-said-what-who-dissed-who-the-first-day-back/>

Page 147: Carraway, Kate. "Rob Ford Is Bananas." *Eye Weekly.* August 18, 2010. <http://www.eyeweekly.com/requiredreading/article/99655>

Page 148: Hannon, Gerald. "Mr. Popular: Why Rob Ford's Winning Over Toronto." *Toronto Life.* September 29, 2010. <http://www.torontolife.com/daily/informer/from-print-edition-informer/2010/09/29/mr-popular-why-rob-ford-winning-over-toronto/?page=3>

Page 149: Hannon, Gerald. "Mr. Popular: Why Rob Ford's Winning Over Toronto." *Toronto Life.* September 29, 2010. <http://www.torontolife.com/daily/informer/from-print-edition-informer/2010/09/29/mr-popular-why-rob-ford-winning-over-toronto/?page=3>

Page 150: Hannon, Gerald. "Mr. Popular: Why Rob Ford's Winning Over Toronto." *Toronto Life.* September 29, 2010. <http://www.torontolife.com/daily/informer/from-print-edition-informer/2010/09/29/mr-popular-why-rob-ford-winning-over-toronto/?page=3>

Page 151: Hannon, Gerald. "Mr. Popular: Why Rob Ford's Winning Over Toronto." *Toronto Life.* September 29, 2010. <http://www.torontolife.com/daily/informer/from-print-edition-informer/2010/09/29/mr-popular-why-rob-ford-winning-over-toronto/?page=3>

Page 152: Alcoba, Natalie. "Don Cherry Blasts 'Left-Wing Pinko' Media at Toronto Mayor's Swearing-In." *National Post.* December 7, 2010. <http://www.canada.com/story_print.html?id=3941641&sponsor=>